PRAISE FOR *ORBITAL PATHS*

Richard Meyer's poems are a delight to read. Their rich language and metrical music draw us in, and give form to a wild and imaginative journey of ideas. These poems are both earthy and celestial, and the poet's eye moves easily from wash hanging on the clothesline to meteors screaming through space. Anchoring it all is a cosmic sense of humor. The effect is enchanting.

> —John Thavis, *New York Times* bestselling author of
> *The Vatican Diaries*

Richard Meyer's generous collection—it's ample enough for two collections or, in Philip Larkin's case, three!—teems with wit and well-tuned songs. There are lines and rhymes, such as these on the subject of time passing, that Cole Porter would have deemed de-lovely: "a *was*, an *is*, and maybe a *when* / the fleeting *now* becomes a *then*." Meyer's poems confront science with belief, thought with feeling, earth with spirit, and staunchness with uncertainty. To upend Robert Frost's adage, his companionable poems begin in wisdom and end in delight. His serious concerns—at the heart of such poems as "The Autumn Way," his striking elegy for Gertrude Klugherz Meyer—affect us more deeply for their alternation with moments of hilarity: "Shall I compare thee to a summer's day? / Mosquitoes. Rain. Vacation without pay." There are too many of these winning moments to count. *Orbital Paths* is chockablock with signal pleasures, and reading it leaves one enlivened and renewed.

> —David Yezzi, author of *Birds of the Air*

Richard Meyer's *Orbital Paths* is a big book in both scope and heart. He addresses abiding themes of love and death and destiny in poems that are sometimes humorous, sometimes grave, and over and over again striking for the directness of their aim—answering what may puzzle or confound us about being human with a well-crafted, sympathetic music.

> —Richard Robbins, Professor of English and Director
> of Creative Writing at Minnesota State University,
> author of *Radioactive City* and *Other Americas*

With surprises that rattle Shakespeare and Donne with jollity, *Orbital Paths* by Richard Meyer is a poetic transformation. Meyer demonstrates an unsurpassed mastery of purpose and form. Defying the predictable rhymes and easy turns that can sometimes sink formal poetry, Meyer reinvents the familiar with updated insight on traditional concerns: sex, creation, mythology, religion, relationships, and nature. Funny and cutting on each page, consider how he uses the image of a monkey stupidly falling from a canopy to move into a damning assessment of how far and then how backward our species has gone in "The Descent of Man."

> An ape fell off its family tree,
> then stood upright on spindly limbs
> and moved around bipedally,
> which led to better hands and thumbs
> and bigger brains, and you and me
> with culture, art, and atom bombs.

Meyer personifies the two best qualities of poets. He sees everything, and he elects (or creates) the perfect word for the exact sentiment he means to convey. So much so, that even when a poem doesn't contain a single word, as in "A Life," the trusting reader goes along challenged, excited, and edified.

I'm partial to winter poems and poetic music, and so it's no surprise that my favorite poem is "Minneopa Falls: January."

> In winter
> the waterfall
> becomes a whale:
> inert, vertical,
> balancing on its tail…

Just listen to that.
Meyer is a siren. Just try to put this collection down.

> —Nicole Helget, author of *Wonder at the Edge of the World, Stillwater,* and *The Summer of Ordinary Ways*

Orbital Paths is, by turns, a showcase of finely crafted, jewel-like poems of epigrammatic concision and glorious wit, and expansive poems of meditation and mythmaking. It orbits in the gravity of dimensions as infinite as the universe itself, highlighting cosmological and existential mysteries, mysticism, questions of God, and the whys and hows of being in "our sliver of eternity." In Richard Meyer's capable hands, there is deft tension between irreverence and homage, sacrilege and supplication, passion and wistfulness, design and happenstance. This is a seasoned debut collection that smoothly melds science, religion, nature and the quotidian with wit and protean intelligence to achieve original insights and cosmic fun.

—Alexander Pepple, Editor, *Able Muse*

Whether expansive or tartly terse, the poems in Richard Meyer's *Orbital Paths* are not afraid to tackle the big themes or converse with the great works. They pay deep attention to nature of various kinds: the human, and the heavenly, and especially the earthy and earthbound—an attention we should treasure, since even now it seems to be passing from the language. These are poems that remember, to use Rhina Espaillat's phrase, "to sing and not to mumble" and that comfort and satisfy with their lucid thought and clear music.

—Maryann Corbett, author of *Breath Control, Credo for the Checkout Line in Winter*, and *Mid Evil*

Richard Meyer is a formalist who knows the power of small things. A three beat line. A quatrain. A cup of tea. In his first collection, *Orbital Paths*, Meyer conjures the cosmos in his garden, explicating the ineffable, describing the soul in comforting, nebulous certainties. Sly, sharp, and deeply human with the humor that suggests, Meyer's poems bring their own durability to the antique forms into which they breathe life and from which they take flight.

—Rick Mullin, author of *Sonnets from the Voyage of the Beagle*

From love to death to our place in the cosmos, Richard Meyer leaves no thorny subject unexplored in this often mesmerizing collection. By turns playful and dark (and sometimes both), he puts a fresh spin on common experience, and gets fresh with the likes of Donne, Marvell, and Dickinson as he riffs on poems from the Western canon. Perhaps his greatest gift is his knack for arresting figures of speech: A field "sweats stones/as I sweat salt." A woodpecker becomes a military inspector. Ardor is "a barrowful of hope/ balanced on a single wheel." The human race, marooned in a "vast and bare" universe, mirrors a man lying alone in a bed meant for two. Here's hoping that in our not-so-bare corner of space, Meyer will get the many readers he deserves.

—Melissa Balmain, Editor, *Light* poetry magazine, and author of *Walking in on People*

Witty, lightly philosophical, sonically pleasurable, Richard Meyer's poems will bring special joy to those with a taste for traditional verse. Yet Meyer is a man of our time, full of doubt and wonder as he gazes at the stars that are the subject of many of the poems. True, he often finds a loneliness in a universe rendered cold by science and modernity. He locates solace, however, in the creativity of the natural world and in poetry itself, "where something comes from nothing all the time." These are poems to be read aloud and savored.

—David M. Katz, author of *Stanzas on Oz, Claims of Home,* and *The Warrior in The Forest*

Orbital Paths by Richard Meyer is a lyrical meditation that sends the reader on a spiritual trajectory into the farthest reaches of the cosmos then firmly back to earth, the panoply of human emotions underpinning the journey. His parodies are utterly delightful, as are the poems dedicated to the natural world. The witty and ingenious epigram, however, is his forte. I would recommend *Orbital Paths* on "Fieldstone" alone.

—Catherine Chandler, author of *Lines of Flight* and *Glad and Sorry Seasons*

Common sense has a poetry all its own: the undeniability of what is shared. And sense-in-common is the quiet measure and balance of these straightforwardly poetic appeals to what is always more, but not *too* much more, than apparent. There are wings here, and sky; but never at the expense of feet, and ground.

—R. Nemo Hill, author of *When Men Bow Down*

There is in Richard Meyer's poetry a refreshing refusal to cater to this culture's fatuous optimism. It isn't the cynical act of the *faux*-jaded young man, nor the sneer of the nihilist, but rather a mature, reflective voice that knows that there is mostly empty space between stars, between places, and between people. Meyer's poems, while firmly atheistic, nevertheless hold out the hope that, through human imagination, "there must be a single telling light."

> —Quincy R. Lehr, author of *The Dark Lord of the Tiki Bar* and *Heimat*

Richard Meyer's poetry covers a lot of ground: history, science, literature, nature, love—it's all here in *Orbital Paths*. But the best news is that these poems are just plain FUN to read. I found myself reading his poems out loud, enjoying his mastery of the craft. I suggest you buy this book, pull up a chair next to the metaphorical, or real, woodstove, and do the same. Like the narrator in his poem "Road Trip," you can't help but "pick up speed and hum along."

> —Robert Crawford, author of *The Empty Chair*

Orbital Paths, Richard Meyer's poetry collection, takes you on a wide-ranging and fascinating ride. Heads up when you travel this road. There's surprise at every turn, and around some corners you may run into yourself. Many of these poems sparkle with delightful humor, and in some the clever wit casts a dark shadow. From backyard birds to frozen waterfalls to a gun toting god, these carefully constructed, accessible poems will entertain and enlighten.

> —Edward Micus, author of *The Infirmary*

These spare and carefully crafted poems are the works of an observer and reflector, a thoughtful and deliberate and yet humorous man, and the consistent voice — often in rhyme, often pared to the bones of the poem, often beautiful in its precision and simplicity — mirrors a poet who still lives in the house in which he was born. "Her bedroom window, black as Minnesota soil," he writes of a dying mother. Whether speaking of love and lost love, or of the sometimes harsh Minnesota climate, or intersections of faith and science, Meyer's poetry artfully shares with us the public comments of a private man.

> —Michael Cantor, author of *Life in the Second Circle*

Richard Meyer's poems, both those in traditional meter and rhyme, and those in free verse, range from the earth below to the heavens above. Inclusive as they are, many exhibit a sparkling, ironic wit and a self-deprecating humor. "Parallel Reverberations," a group of playful literary parodies from Christopher Marlowe to Robert Frost, skillfully imitates the diction and tone of the original pieces, and Meyer's shorter poems often display the compression of a latter-day Emily Dickinson and leave readers reflecting on their own humanity.

—Jerome Zuckerman, Professor Emeritus of English, Minnesota State University

Insightful and sure-footed throughout, *Orbital Paths* contains potent genies in small bottles, and heady pleasures. Meyer's mastery of the short poem will stand the test of time.

—Ed Shacklee, poet and public defender

Humility and boldness mark *Orbital Paths* as a classic collection. Meyer submits to the ultimate realities—solitude, space, sex, love, death, beauty, sin, the divine—but with Promethean boldness captures them afresh, demanding nothing less than perfection in his poetic form. He dares to join Dickinson, Yeats, and Frost in the great lyric tradition of confronting the human situation in a precise music of wit and feeling. He understands the labor required to achieve simplicity and sincerity, and willingly pays the price.

—William Carpenter, poet and lawyer

Orbital Paths

poems by

Richard Meyer

ScienceThrillers Media

SCIENCETHRILLERS MEDIA

www.ScienceThrillersMedia.com
Publisher@ScienceThrillersMedia.com

First edition, 2015

Library of Congress Control Number 2015943392

POE005010 POETRY / American / General
POE023030 POETRY / Subjects & Themes / Nature

ISBN 978-1-940419-07-7 (hardcover)
ISBN 978-1-940419-08-4 (trade paperback)
ISBN 978-1-940419-09-1 (ebook)

Cover by Ian Koviak, The Book Designers (www.bookdesigners.com)

How fortunate I am to have been born
in this time and place, and into this family—

for my parents, *Gert and Andy,*

and my seven siblings:

Betsy

Mike

Tony

Mark

Annie

Josie

Sep

And 'tis a pretty toy to be a poet.

— Christopher Marlowe

Orbital Paths

Contents

I. Event Horizons

II. Orbital Paths

III. Terrestrial Matters

I

Event Horizons

Marooned

The universe is vast and bare—
a vacuum—mostly empty space
with matter scattered here and there
around a stranded human race.

Kept quarantined by time and place,
we languish in the light-year sea
and scan horizons for a trace
of life, or mind, or deity.

Stars slowly transit overhead,
distant cousins of the sun.
I roll onto my side in bed,
a bed too cold and wide for one.

Singularity

Before the beginning, prior to God,
the nothing that wasn't isn't so odd
as all of the something suddenly here,
no matter whatever made it appear.

Adrift

The Milky Way's a turning wheel
    of blazing spheres of light,
thick nested suns that gleam and reel
    and spiral through the night.

When seen from far away by God,
    if there's a God to look,
it's just a faint and hazy pod,
    a bubble in a brook,

a twinkling microscopic spot
    far off the cosmic shore,
one commonplace galactic dot
    amid a billion more—

and lost in all this boundless hive
    of misty galaxies
that sometimes perish, sometimes thrive
    across the cosmic seas

we ride this rock that tags behind
    a mediocre star
and use what passes for a mind
    to wonder what we are.

In Time

Time's a wonderful device
so clear   linear   precise

the plot of everything
unraveling like a string—
beginning, middle, end

neat bits and parts
on which we can depend
like beating hearts
an erstwhile friend

a *was*, an *is*, and maybe a *when*
the fleeting *now* becomes a *then*

the past absorbed, weighed down by rocks
the present lost in ticking clocks
the future a door no key unlocks
a tangled Zeno's paradox

the *done*, the *here*, the *yet to come*
a constant flowing to and from

carried by light from distant stars
traveling through the curve of space
sometimes it moves like queued up cars
or waits like roses in a vase

the gone, the going, the what's ahead
never a now that isn't dead

time yesterday and time tomorrow
but never time today
impossible to save or borrow
always on the way

some say it marks a certain point
while others claim it's out of joint
and try their best to set it right

God's pocket watch wound up at night

Let There Be!

The formless void gives rise to solid things,
creating stuff by pulling cosmic strings—

a quantum dance, a conjured pantomime
where something comes from nothing all the time.

Farsighted

Like an old woman picking through her purse,
jabbing at coins for exact change,
the astronomer probes the universe.
Rummaging through the night skies,
up to his elbow in stars,
he pushes past clustered galaxies
and iridescent nebulas.
Always at a further range
his telescopic finger pries,
always deeper in the dark
he stretches an uncertain hand
and squints at what he cannot see.
For such a search the eyes alone won't do.
He must rely on guess, go by feel.
So much is hidden from his view,
so much recedes before his reach
he murmurs under breath, as if in prayer,
and hopes his scientific chant
will charm the delicate instruments.
He knows, based on a calculated faith,
beyond this meager Milky Way
he'll find the cosmic coins that pay.

Road Trip

The static on the radio
preserves creation's primal song—
a steady, crackling, background hiss
repeating *this ... now this ... hear this.*
The road runs on—a stretch to go.
I pick up speed and hum along.

A Telling Light

This very moment other alien races
most likely prosper, perish, or persist
out there in scattered far-off cosmic places.

Dispersed among a pellet spray of suns
sequestered planets secretly resist
all knowledge of the dead or living ones.

But here beneath the spangled vault of night
I lie upon my back and still insist
that there must be a single telling light.

The Pilfered Apple

The two felt pleased,
downright amused—
the snake appeased,
the god confused.

Redemption

Both Christian faith and science fact
demand a sacrificial act—
a forfeit of a cosmic scope
that gives us life and grants us hope.

To form our elemental stuff
two parents coupling aren't enough.
To come to being we require
the selfless deed of something higher.

The wondrous matter that we are
was forged and shaped inside a star—
the crucible for everything,
an immolated offering.
It was a hefty price to pay,
an astral gift from far away.

When feeling hopeless, broken-down,
of no-account, a dolt, a clown,
a worthless mote, consumed by sin—
I flash a self-important grin
and look into the nighttime sky:
That I might live a Sun must die!

First Cause

Some never leave off wondering
if life's a chance or destined thing.
The answer seems quite evident—
we're all a scheduled accident.

Make Ready

Dream pear blossoms, Richard,
and fruit on the stem

though frost strikes the orchard
when spring comes again.

Sleep deep and untortured,
lie hushed in your bed

like those in the churchyard
with stones at their head.

Waterfall in Winter

Cascading from
that craggy lip
it tumbles down
a limestone chest,
the glaucous flow
spreading wide
and coming to rest
at the plunge pool
forty feet below,
where I stand,
a winter soul
alone and shivering
in drifted snow,
looking up
with arms raised
to that solid mass
looming above me,
impassive, green-gray,
severe as God's beard
on Judgment Day.

Morning Alchemy

and floating there
inside my cup
a filigree

the skilled barista
drew for me
but as I looked

it slowly changed
transformed itself
and rearranged

into a tree
with milky limbs
and then a leaf

a bird, a star
and after that
a swirl of snow

I watched the froth
and melting foam
dissolve in golden monochrome

before I lifted to my lip
the longed for metamorphic sip

The Go-Around

On a star-filled carousel,
its spiral arms flung wide
and spinning fast as hell,
we're taken for a ride.

II

Orbital Paths

Communion

The moon's a sacramental host,
night air the eucharistic wine
for those who can't give up the ghost
of finding love incarnadine.

I take the moonlight on my tongue
and drink the linden-blossomed air,
remembering when I was young
and mouthed the same unanswered prayer.

This Morning

A sparrow slams against the pane
with such a pounding-breakneck-thump
I think the picture window split
or cracked into a spider vein.
As often as we hear them hit,
we always shudder, flinch, or jump.
When birds collide with glass and die
they leave a little viscous smear,
but otherwise the view stays clear
that frames a square of trees and sky.

And you, my love, in this warm bed,
a shiver rippled through your blood.
You looked away and winced and yelped
and pressed your fingers into me
when startled by that beak-first thud.
You sorrow for whatever's dead
and dread our own fragility.
Our mortal natures can't be helped,
no more than birds that crash and fall,
mistaking windowpanes for air.
This present moment is our all,
our sliver of eternity.
There's just the now, this now we share
to jointly breathe and live and be.

The sunlight cuts a glaring line
where pleated curtains nearly meet.
A long white beam transects our feet
then angles sharply like a tine
and strikes a blank impassive wall.
Some trinkets on the dresser shine.
Outside the sparrows chirp and dart.
The rising day won't let us stall
much longer in our languid rest,
but for this moment I am blessed
to know your mind and have your heart
and feel your yielding flesh on mine.

A Totem Bird

What else but a sign,
a message with wings,
this mourning dove
that perches above
on the telephone line
and coos and sings
to its absent mate:
I wait, I wait.

Tempted

Forbidden fruit, a rebel will,
the woman's captivating charms—
so Adam faltered, ate his fill
and fell from grace into her arms.

Some still find strength to fall in turn
and follow independent Eve
from whose transgression men may learn
to slough constraint, rise up, conceive.

La Gioconda

This way to the Mona Lisa

Only the tired guard shows no surprise.
With folded arms he leans against a wall
and notes one woman moving through the queue,
a blonde with ample breasts and slender thighs.
The best today, he thinks. *Well built and tall.*

He stutter taps a foot against the floor,
and checks the time, and yawns a little sigh.
To him you're like some criminal of war
condemned and placed on permanent display,
encased in sturdy glass for all to view.
You'll never be released and cannot die.

He stands at ease. He rarely looks your way,
accustomed to the smirk behind his back
and numb to eyes that slice across his neck.

To Eva, Who Clings To Chastity

Why say such ecstasy is vice?
Why label pleasure sin?
Open your gates of paradise
And let my serpent in.

Quandary

For love I willfully undress,
so to the priest I must confess.
With passion quick and penance slow,
between the bed and church I go.

The Allure of Bad Boys

Loki! Loki! wayward lad,
full of mischief, godly bad,
two-faced brother, troubled son,
loveable chameleon,
trickster, charmer, puzzling rune
dark as night and bright as moon,
working magic, hatching schemes,
gorgeous incubus of dreams,
soul of ice and heart of fire,
darling villain—my desire!

Hera's Song

catch him, latch him
grate and grind
crack the whip to make him mind

rein him, train him
scoff and frown
leash him short and wear him down

hold him, scold him
stomp the floor
tame the satyr you adore

A Polished Pome for Heidi

Had Eve not sinned and gone amiss
and Eden's gates been firmly shut,
we wouldn't have this chance to kiss
or the joy of doing you-know-what.

Since I'm a fair, forgiving man
and wish to even up the score,
I give the apple back again
that you may eat it to the core.

Yield to the stirring in your hips,
yield to the pleasant tug of vice—
press Adam's fruit against your lips
and taste the juice of Paradise.

Coiffure

for Lenore

Arranged impossibly about her head,
chimerical, cavorting in air,
a tumbling filigree of hair
all molten golden-red
cascades in curls
and braids and waves and whorls
and flows and falls by its own laws
until it grants a sudden pause
to here or there caress
the fabric of her skin or dress,
like hair that frames the mythic faces
of Botticelli's dancing Graces.

Woman with Chrysanthemums

"One sees as one wishes to see." —Edgar Degas

A burst of blossoms splashing wide,
a woman crowded to the side.

She's seated oddly, and alone,
and simply done in monochrome.

Both dwarfed and driven by the blooms
she's granted only little room,

almost an afterthought, half done,
a contrast to the floral sun.

She sits in secret, we suppose.
An enigmatic smile half shows

behind a strangely gestured hand,
a pose we cannot understand.

And though we wonder for a while
at what she looks or why she smiles,

she never is but always becomes
the woman with chrysanthemums.

Tryst

I've seen the lurid marbled moon
veiled with clouds in a vacant park;
I've seen her climb a hilltop throne
in bridal white and stand alone
against a deeply purpled sky,
her face a bright and cryptic rune.
I've heard her whisper in the dark
that old incantatory lie.

A Former Girlfriend's Spaniel

Her pet was a cocker named Sam
who yipped, "A true canine I am,
but when yet a pup
the vet fixed me up
so I'm neither a mister nor mam."

Ardor

How we labor the heart,
pushing up an angled plank
a barrowful of hope
balanced on a single wheel.

Keeping a truce with gravity and doubt,
we beg that narrow ramp to hold,
pray a knee won't buckle,
a wrist give out.

Dimmicks Beach

When you walk the strand
some afternoon,
past those rocks
and over that dune,
down to the place
where windblown sand
lashed at my face
when I took your hand
and white-maned waves
charged in with a roar
as if to drive us
away from the shore,

ask the sea
if it remembers me.

Morning Tea

Let's take our toast and tea
to the porch. Come, sit with me.

This crackled porcelain cup—
thin, cool as oyster shell
opening out and up
like an inverted bell
in the hand—each finger molds
around it like a weld.
How perfectly it holds,
how delicate when held.

Riding the Red Jacket Trail

Up late into the night,
a room away from me,
you sit alone and write
while sipping Ceylon tea
and conjure with your pen
our afternoon's long ride,

and so with me in sleep
where paths weave into dreams
and stretch for mile on mile
past hills and farms and streams,
but the tandem pace we keep
lasts only for a while.

We pedal the trail again
from town to countryside.
The day is strangely mild.
The phlox has lost its flame,
sumac's rusting red.
Behind a trailside fence
a garden plot's gone wild.

A deer leaps from the ditch
and bounds across a field
half-harvested of corn.
We pass a weathered barn,
its roof and walls collapsed,
then cross a trestle bridge
spanning a steep ravine

and trace a river's edge
that leads into some woods,
a tunneling of trees,
the fretwork canopy
shot through with stippled light.

A quaking aspen sheds
a basketful of leaves.
Like whiffling yellow moths
they flutter over you.
A bird you cannot name
calls out to you in song,
a sudden flash of wings
hurries you along.

Something in you swerves.
I cannot see your face.
Full spate in headlong flight
you lose me at a curve
that skirts a railroad track.
The wind gives you a push
and you outdistance me
without a backward look.

We ride Red Jacket Trail
together, yet apart.

I roll onto my side
and reach out in the dark
in a bed that feels too wide.
Each breath's a push and pull
as tidal as the sea,
each rasping in my throat
a strangled syllable,
a suffocated plea.

A window lets in night,
moonlight bars the floor.
You staunch the spill of words
black-puddling on a page,
then step into the hall
and listen at my door
like someone near a cage.
A stairway's on your right.

And out beyond the town
a trail divides and turns.
The moon is going down,
the evening star still burns.

The paths within a house
(like those that etch the land)
lengthen, branch, and bend
and take a winding course
to their uncertain end.

Point of Interest

along the scenic byway near Blackduck, Minnesota

A forest road cuts through the birch and pine
where continental watersheds divide,
a place of lakes where streams and rivers start.

We stop the car and pose before a sign,
tethered arm to arm, tugging side to side
against a slope that's tilting us apart.

Fault Line

You lying on your side, and I on mine,
both turned away in darkness, spine to spine—
each back a knotted ridge, the space between
a rift, a trench, a mute dividing line.

One Winter

Where are the snows of years gone by?
And where's the one who came this way
beneath a low and chalky sky
and walked with me that winter day

down hillside woods, past limestone walls,
then up a creek bed deep in snow
to see the frozen waterfalls?
The cataract's arrested flow

shone like a pillared mound of glass,
all plunge and roar solidified
into a looming blue-green mass.
We stood in silence, side by side,

and winter held us, kept us bound
in consonance like ice and stone,
and laced together on the ground
the only tracks were ours alone.

But lives are fluid, mutable,
not fixed tableaux inside a sphere
where worlds are snowy beautiful
and nothing changes year to year.

I saw that winter melt and go
in icy currents down a stream
and all that bright beguiling snow
become a lost dissolving dream.

House Cleaning

Along with dust and lint,
in corners, on a chair
or book or window vase
I find your random trace
in remnant strands of hair
or a smudged fingerprint.

A Blessing

like water, flow away
like wind, blow away
into the world, go away

unhinged, on the wing
a winsome feathered thing
splayed heart unraveling

artful, vagrant, free
uprooted, far from me
outlander, refugee

III

Terrestrial Matters

The Descent of Man

An ape fell off its family tree,
then stood upright on spindly limbs
and moved around bipedally,
which led to better hands and thumbs
and bigger brains, and you and me
with culture, art, and atom bombs.

Anima

The periodic table
sufficiently explains
how elements are able
to manufacture brains
or fabricate a heart.
That's the easy part.

The soul's another matter.
Here science comes up mute
and speculations shatter.
There's nothing to compute,
no tools to measure with.
For this, we turn to myth.

Red Splendor

In the crabapple tree in the garden
birds eat of the bountiful fruit,

little red pomes, lush and plump
like thickly clustered berries.

Cardinals, robins, waxwings
glide in for an easy feast

no deity forbids,
although in wild fermented flight

against the trickery of glass
a few of them will fall.

Primordial Weather

Extremities—the hot and cold—
two desert regions, one of snow
and one of sand (as we are told
by experts in geology)
were very different long ago,
a hundred million years or so.

The parched Sahara used to be
a great and rolling ancient sea,
a liquid realm of frothy brine
where waves rose up like drifting dunes
and stretched to each horizon line
without a hint of solid land.
An eon's worth of suns and moons
shone on the ocean's crinkled face,
and the wind flung with a mighty hand
a salty spray that hissed like sand.

Antarctica was wet and hot:
a steamy, stifling, sticky place
of rampant green and jungle rot,
and nothing glared a glacial white
except the stars and moon at night,
or clouds by day, or crashing surf—
a landscape drenched in sun and rain,
a wilderness of ferns, the turf
of reptiles, bugs, and proto-birds
and dinosaurs that roamed in herds.

The mind can hardly entertain
the sweep of time and drastic change
presented in a science book.
The process is too vast and strange.

But if we take an inward look
we witness similar extremes
when inner climates shift and turn,
though unlike worlds or hemispheres
we don't need geologic years.
In moments we can switch, it seems,
from moods that freeze to moods that burn.

How easily we flip the page
from icy apathy to rage,
from calm to storm and back again,
and all within a narrow span.
The weather formed in human hearts
operates by fits and starts.
We're seldom in a steady state.
Consider how we love and hate.

Apollonian Hymn

reason's a planner and pauser
the master restrainer and causer
the rudder, the anchor, the hawser

Sisyphus

The doomed, tormented Sisyphus
stuck on a rutted hill in hell
may curse the gods that cursed him thus
but cannot break the binding spell.
His bootless labor without end
can only make the rock descend.

Yet this defiant mortal sneers
and spits upon the trampled soil.
He grants no vengeful god his fears
nor calls condemned his ceaseless toil.
He battles demon rock and hill
because he thinks to win by will.

The Great Builders

The Pyramids were built on bread and beer
and China's Wall on bowls of rationed rice.
The human cost was markedly severe,
but mighty rulers shrugged and paid the price.

A Life

!
)
)ABC123
)/
)?
)$
);
) &)'
)~)':)!)'!)?
((' . . .
(. .
(\
[(]
.

A Verse

for someone or other

an insignificant speck
largely alive below the neck
not so much between the ears
around for roughly eighty years

Forbidden Fruits

Some say, according to belief,
that God forbids us to eat beef,
while others claim with equal zeal
that pork is an unholy meal.
And there are those who swear it sin
to sample wine or beer or gin.
From east to west the world around
we're warned forbidden fruits abound.
The globe is filled from pole to pole
with wrangling creeds that seek my soul.
They plow a straight and narrow road
and pave it with their moral code.
They tell us what to eat and drink,
and after that what we should think.
Although I haven't seen their light
and saved my soul from endless night,
these ministers of right and wrong
have helped to move my doubt along.
I've learned a worthwhile thing or two
from masters of the do-not-do:
We must indeed watch what we chew
and swallow down and take as true.

Disputation

Relentless waves collapse against the rocks
that wall a jagged, undiminished shore.
The water seems undone by granite blocks,
and yet each wasted wave is followed up with more.
Undaunted water rolls, and rolls, and rolls on in.
Both rock and wave contest where land and sea begin,
and both display their might, and both are always right.
The ancient quarrel roars and howls all day, all night.

The Penitent

I tied a cincture round my heart
and cloistered it a world away
where it was humbled night and day,
a wizened little monk in gray.

But it was willful from the start
and spurned the halo-tonsured head,
the coarse unbuttered daily bread,
the lonely, cold, and narrow bed.

At length it could not play the part
and shed the cowl and sackcloth shirt
to feel again the thrill and hurt
of flesh and breath and sweat and dirt.

Recipe

a corrugated brain
an insufficient heart
one postulated soul

combine and mix to start
season, marinate, strain
then mold into a whole

Unschooled

To parse a paragraph of woods
or diagram the hills
demands a grammar of the wise
beyond my simple skills.

In town I'm competent and cool,
reciting rules of thumb—
but stand abashed in nature's school,
illiterate—and dumb.

Something Like Worms

"and he was eaten of worms, and gave up the ghost"
—Acts 12:23

it must be something like worms
that get inside the head, larvae hatched
in batches from little bullet-shaped eggs

laid by some winged dark thing,
maggots wriggling beneath the skull,
the brain a three-pound tub of lard gone bad

and the fat white worms squirming and burrowing
through gray corrugations soft as grease,
each a mouth at the end of an eating tube,

blind and deaf, eating their way out,
eating the alphabet, eating your name,
eating words, eating *pillow, mother, blue*

eating sun and moon and stars,
gorging on everything that isn't worm
until they burst from chest, belly, and balls

into a world where no one and nothing
is innocent, and a finger becomes a worm
curled around a trigger

October Closing

The red and yellow tents come down,
the trapeze sky turns gray,
a lagging harlequin in brown
looks back and walks away.

Inspection

Picoides villosus: the hairy woodpecker

Smartly dressed,
sentry straight,
he tours every day—

this bird in black
with white lapels
who wears a red beret.

He corkscrew climbs
the nervous trees
standing at attention.

Aloof—precise—
his urgent eyes
conduct a close inspection.

That needle nose,
a brash baton,
notes every crease and cuff.

Mechanical
as marching feet,
with gestures quick and stiff,

he pokes and pries
from hedge to fence
until he's seen enough.

Without salute
or slightest nod
this colonel swaggers off.

Then leaves relax,
and shadows breathe,
and sparrows dare to speak—

a dear relief
from scrutiny
invested with a beak.

Indian Summer

The sun is burning borrowed wood,
the sky's an azure fraud—
a late October sleight-of-hand
that awes an easy crowd.

They Come Back

The slow river bends
like an elbow, turns
north, scores the valley,
its long smooth largo
keeping time and place.

Wind plucks the trees, pulls
leaves from maple, ash
and oak, scatters them
in swirls, churns the piles
yellow, ocher, brown.

Starlings pitch and wheel,
scrawling their flurried
notes across gray sky.
Dust clouds lift from cut
fields, drift into town.

Fog hangs in streets and
alleys, wraps around
houses, pools beneath
a yellow yard-light,
lingers near a porch.

They come back: a face,
a faint voice, a hand
reaching through the haze.
Sometimes, in soft bronze
weather, they come back.

Late November

Not a cloud or wisp of cloud
ruffles the wide unwrinkled sky
stretched tight as a blue scrim.

Trees stand bare and mute,
each leaf played out, a fallen note
in this quiet concert hall.

Intermission.

Somewhere in a large white room
another orchestra tunes up.

The Mongrel

I always hear him on my daily walk,
howling with a kind of human shout
inside a fence behind that gray-stone house
where no one seems to enter or come out.

Sometimes I glimpse a length of chain, a dark
and frantic eye or hank of matted hair.
Far down the street, above the city noise,
his wailing follows, lacerating air.

Christmas Trees

They are a foremost symbol of the season—
these trees we bring indoors and decorate
in splendor suited for a potentate.
We may not know the meaning or the reason
a common pine is granted such a show,
except to say tradition tells us so.

Some folks, the up-to-date unorthodox,
have opted for the manufactured way
and in their living rooms put on display
those snap-together pieces from a box,
green plastic branches uniformly bent
with built-in lights and artificial scent.

The purist searches, sparing no expense,
for sturdy specimens of conifer.
In parking lots of captive spruce and fir
he finds them hobbled, leaning on a fence,
or tightly bound in nets and lying down,
stacked high on flatbed trailers brought to town.

A tree well-tinseled, trimmed, and set aglow
gives customary holiday delight,
and yet how often I prefer the sight
of evergreens deep rooted where they grow.
In unadorned simplicity they stand,
and lacking ostentation seem more grand.

I like to see them lined up in a row
or bunched in groups that hug a summer hill,
or on a winter morning, cold and still,
and plainly dressed in dappled coats of snow.
I like them in a yard or in a park
and wearing just their needles and their bark.

Onslaught

The sky crowds closer than it should
and ruptures with its weight.
All day the scudding clouds unload
raw tons of powdered freight.

A sullen bellows in the north
grows petulant and rude,
then hurls its swirling glacial wrath
to lower latitudes.

Glum sparrows button up their coats
and hunch on chimney stacks.
The elms complain about the cold
with stiff and creaking backs.

Each house draws deep within its walls
and holds its timbers tight.
The town is wrapped in linen shrouds,
the world rubs out in white.

But all this ominous display
is merely idle threat—
a surly January day
that April will forget.

No Sanctuary

This January sky blue as June
doesn't move the sparrows.
They hunker down, little gargoyles
braced against the wind,
feather-puffed and patient,
doing gray penance
in a snow-stuccoed hedge.

Minneopa Falls: January

"Very like a whale." —Hamlet

In winter
the waterfall
becomes a whale:
inert, vertical,
balancing on its tail
from plunge pool
to rock lip,
petrified carcass
caught mid-leap
in a dazzling breach,
pinned by flukes
and flippers
there's no backing down
now and here's
an end to up,
part of its great bulk
stuck against stone,
the rest hanging
paralyzed in air
where all flow
and song and mist
congeal and harden
to a crystal monolith.

March

The woods exhale a mist,
hillsides catch the sun.
Beneath its pitted crust
a creek begins to run.

Along a drifted hedge
girdled branches show
where hungry rabbits fed
when it was twelve below.

Atop the backyard shed
a ridge of tattered snow
dissolves around its edge
and takes the melting slow.

The brittle sheet of ice
puddled beneath a spout
thaws and freezes twice
before the weekend's out.

Naked trees cast down
a tracery of shade
across a patchwork yard
mottled white and brown.

The ground is working hard
to come back from the dead
and soften for the spade
that turns a garden bed.

Squizzer

It
could
almost be
a taxidermic trick
tacked four feet up the basswood tree:
rigid as rock,
nose downward,
legs and toes splayed,
head cocked back a click;
it's a glass-eyed stub,
an alert nub, a gnarl
on the trunk,
ossified, inert, a seamless stitching
of fur to bark,
but

that

long

tail is

a gray

nerve

twitching!

Unseasonable

April is a foolish farmer
to think that he can sow
a second crop of winter
by casting seeds of snow.

Sunday Morning in June

Arched branches catch the slanting light,
maple leaves brighten like bits of green glass.

Toast and coffee wait on the back porch table,
familiar morning gifts
set out in a screen vestibule.

The lawn, a deep green nave vaulted in blue,
stops abruptly at the alley, a simple T
traced in grass and gravel.

From the neighbor's kitchen window
the clink of a spoon in a cereal bowl
pings like an altar bell, little silver notes
chiming through the high hedge.

A robin splashes in the birdbath,
sprays a blessing of water drops.
Finches and common sparrows
congregate at the feeders.

Pulsing red on a telephone wire, a cardinal
calls out the good news.
The mixed choir chirps and whistles.

A squirrel, stoop-shouldered and gray,
sermonizes from an ash limb.
Peonies kneel at a garden fence,
bow their thick, perfumed heads.

And the faint *clink clink clink* of metal on china
rings again, like a bell announcing matins.

Tendrils

They grow together, dense and green
in rampant woodland underbrush
part visible and part unseen—
they grow together, wild and lush,
as coiling leaf and root combine
where light and shadow intertwine.

Fireflies

1

They pulse with golden light
in garden beds,
along the hedge,
grass low or shoulder height.

A simple summer rite—
to sit and watch
on a dark porch
as they punctuate the night.

2

a blip, a blink, a random spark,
a yellow glimmer in the dark

an amber flicker, bold and clear,
a calling out that says *I'm here*

3

They have their silent say
in blinking yellow light
and abdicate the day
for necessary night.

Passer Domesticus

the common house sparrow, also called the English sparrow

They dress in frowzy jackets,
they twitter strident tongues—
unduly coarse in most respects,
mere balls of lint with wings.

They do not mind a gutter,
a chimney pot or eave;
they loiter through inclement weather
without the sense to leave.

They roister in the roads,
they litter every lawn;
their shanties ruin neighborhoods,
they inundate the town.

They squabble over crumbs,
they lack civility—
to feed and fight and fornicate
their sole philosophy.

Promiscuous and rude,
they wrangle, loaf, and beg—
this rabble of the English brood,
plebeians from the egg.

Fieldstone

I look across a broken field
that spills its rubbled glacial yield.
This farm that's rocky to a fault,
where the ground sweats stones as I sweat salt,
insists my hands get boulder worn
before it gives up beans or corn.

The Clothesline

Underwear hides on the middle wire,
flanked by sheets, long towels, overalls.
Three checkered housedresses pinned at the shoulders
face the neighbor's yard, puff outward in the wind,
lift their hems to apple trees across the picket fence.
In a hodgepodge cotton frieze, socks toe the outer line.

The hands that hang this washing remember
putting up cloth diapers to dry and whiten in the sun,
two dozen every day in good weather.
Rain or winter meant ropes slung below
the basement ceiling, the wet load sagging and dripping
like a platoon of surrender flags.

Two old people don't dirty much. A small laundry basket
once a week maybe, if it's not a Monday for bedding.
The lifting gets heavier, the reaching harder these days.
This clothesline has outlasted her back and arms.
When she said she wanted one, her husband made it himself,
welded steel tubing set in concrete footings.

Spring air brings the sweet talcum scent of lilacs
into the yard and robins fat with eggs.
She snaps wrinkles from a pillowcase, whistles
an old tune, a scrap of cradlesong. It's a good drying day.
And when she fastens towels corner to corner
with wooden clothespins, she's back hanging diapers again.

The Clothesline

IV

Shooting Stars

Shooting Stars

God was shooting stars for fun,
just killing time in idle play
one tedious eternal day.
He used his finger for a gun—
an index pistol .44
that rent the heavens with a roar
and carried quite a cosmic kick.
He liked its heft, he liked the sound
each time he fired off a round.
And he was more than lightning quick
snapping the handgun from his hip.

In a deft display of marksmanship
he drilled six bullets into space
at such a rapid-fire pace
they sounded like a single shot.
He raised the gun to his lower lip
and blew a smoking fingertip,
then saw six dazzling stars explode
and vanish in a spray of sparks

that died and left an inky blot,
a gaping hole where nothing glowed.
As targets stars were easy marks.
God laughed and started to reload.

He fired with a steady rate
and blasted multitudes at whim.
Each shattered like a china plate
or vanished in a chalky puff.
No star was fair or bright enough
nor insignificant and dim
to merit amnesty from him.
He shot a zigzag bullet track
along the gleaming Zodiac,
and all the starlit cosmos felt
the imprint of his shooting spree.

He blew away Orion's belt
and made the Southern Cross a T.
Canis Major lost an eye
and mighty Hercules a knee.
He gelded Taurus, trimmed a horn.
Pollux staggered, reeled and dropped
like fireworks that fall and die,
while brother Castor stood forlorn,
bereft and tilting in the sky.
Steadfast Polaris flared and popped.
Next brilliant Betelgeuse was gone,
then gone the Dipper, Ram, and Crown,
and gone the graceful long-necked Swan.

The clustered Pleiades rained down
like bits of shattered crockery.
God smiled and fired on and on
with deconstructive artistry.

As constellations fell apart,
new forms emerged and took on shape:
The Hangman's Tree, The Weeping Heart,
The Whip, The Spear, The Walking Ape,
The Tangled Web, The Beak & Claw,
The Anvil and The Tiger Paw,
and Gorgon, and Leviathan.
And here and there a vagrant sun
thrown from its customary place
wandered outcast and alone,
an orphaned derelict in space.

In patchwork fashion with his gun
God kept on putting out the light
star by star and sun by sun,
creating random swaths of night.
He fired standing, kneeling, prone,
behind his back, from side to side,
and double-handed on the run.
And stars exploded far and wide
in bursts of bright oblivion,
and all the heavens shook and shone
in pyrotechnic loveliness—
a privileged view from where he stood.
God saw his work and said, *That's Good!*

He was a crack-shot deity,
a pistolero to be feared
who brought the stars down handily.
They dropped in droves; nevertheless,
the teeming galaxies appeared
as thickly nested as before,
for there were stars and stars galore.
The boundless cosmos glowed with light.
As far and deep as he could see
the black was balanced by the white,
and alternating day and night
kept ticking through eternity.
So many stars. They numbered more
than bullets in his bandolier.
For all the ammunition spent
his salvos barely made a dent
across the vast celestial sphere.

Just one more shot, God said aloud,
and then I'll take a break and rest.
He scanned the starry gallery
and spied a far galactic cloud.
With gutsy confidence he chose
the smallest pixel he could see
inside that hazy, swarming nest.
He struck a wide-stance shooter's pose,
scratched his grizzled beard and spit.
He flexed a hand. The knuckles cracked.
His gaze became a snake-eyed slit.

This wondrous stunt, this closing act
would constitute a stellar trick,
a gunman's fitting epilogue—
like snuffing out a candlewick
at eighty paces in a fog.
He flashed a grin, then cocked his thumb
and made a little clucking sound
to simulate a hammer click.
A double-loaded magnum round
sat chambered in the cylinder.
He pointed at the distant blur
and set the v-notch on the dot—
that trembling star, a paltry crumb
of hydrogen and helium.
God pulled the trigger, took the shot.

Damn me! he growled. *I can't have missed.*
That bullet must've been a dud!
But miss he did. A twitching wrist
and frenzy burning in the blood
had thrown his aim off by a hair.
The errant bullet passed so near
it brushed that star's corona sphere
and sparked an arcing solar flare.
When speeding by it whined and hissed.
Beneath a bristling beetle-brow
God's glaring eyes were fixed like tacks
upon the sun he missed somehow.
That little star still twinkled there,

returning God's long-distance stare,
and blithely hopping side to side
it danced the dance of parallax.

God's daring long-shot missed its mark
and sailed into the outer dark,
but by the laws of cosmic math
that little miss was magnified
and put the bullet on a path
which sent it soaring light years wide.

With peak velocity it sped
past galaxy and galaxy
(some shifted blue, some shifted red)
like islands in an endless sea
then grazed a quasar, ricocheted
and kept that course until it strayed
and punched a long and hollow trail
straight through a Horsehead Nebula—
then clipped a roving comet's tail,
angled past Andromeda
and tumbled toward a milky disc,
a far-off spiral asterisk
with spokes curled round its central bar.

Followed by a tracer track
the bullet came in hard and fast
and slammed into a humdrum star
that towed nine planets in its wake.

The massive cataclysmic blast
scorched the solar system black
and brought an end to God's mistake.

Around that standard yellow sun
a minor world—the third one out—
(the home of *Homo sapiens,*
an upright creature with a mind
as by that species self-defined)
had carved a stable solar route.

Beyond the dust and thick debris
above the cinder-ball of Earth
(once marbled green and blue and brown)
with nothing there alive to see,
a constellation called The Clown
rose slowly in the eastern sky.
With a bulbous nose and twinkling eye
it blinked and winked with cosmic mirth
and kept a fixed and doltish grin
as asteroids whizzed by its chin,
then turned a clumsy somersault
against the heavens' speckled vault
and hung there smiling, upside-down,
and held that acrobatic pause
as would a prankster of renown
awaiting thunderous applause.

V

Parallel Reverberations

Blind Date

after Shakespeare

Shall I compare thee to a summer's day?
Mosquitoes. Rain. Vacation without pay.

Waist Deep

after Henry Wadsworth Longfellow

The tide rises, the tide falls.
It shrinks my cock, contracts my balls,
Makes me shiver, goose-bumped and blue.
The waves churn up a frothy stew,
      And the tide rises, the tide falls.

Slimy seaweed coils and crawls
Around my legs, catches my balls;
A laughing gull swoops down at me,
Dead fish things wash up from the sea,
      And the tide rises, the tide falls.

Someone from the beach house calls;
I wade toward shore, cupping my balls.
A long dark shape and angled fin
Shadow me as I'm heading in.
      And the tide rises, the tide falls.

Dawdling After Wordsworth

after William Wordsworth

I wandered lonely as a cloud
    Across a sullen sky
Until the evening wrung me out
    And hung me up to dry.

The past is parent of the now
    And breeds more misery,
And recollection, I have found,
    Brings no tranquility.

To Helen: A Working Girl at *The Palace*

after Christopher Marlowe

Hers is no face to launch a thousand ships
or start a siege of harbor wall and tower,
yet men contend to anchor at her hips
and pay in cash to sack her by the hour.

Person, Place, Thing

after Shakespeare

What's in a name? the nimble poet asks.
How like that sly linguistic acrobat
asserting words are arbitrary masks
which may be switched at whim from this to that.

It's quite phenomenal to say a rose
by any other name would smell as nice.
The names of things are their essential clothes.
What good are words if they are not precise?

Altar Call

after John Donne

Go to it. Collar him. Catch another one.
Take him in the apse, past the confession booth,
where stained light ignites a martyred youth.
Make him kneel, open mouthed. Do it and be done.

Compel him to surrender, yield, obey,
to learn by rote what he's supposed to say,
just like the *Confiteor* and *Kyrie*.
Demand he linger after Mass today.

Have him in the rectory. Press him hard
and long. Constrain, shatter him. Fill his holes
with your indulgences. Leave him scarred,
ruined, bruised. Drop him in your well of souls.

Strip, bend, break him now. Your will be done,
in the name of the father's ghostly son.

The Way To Wealth

an old adage amended

There are no gains
without the pains
of some in chains.

Solicitation: Love in the Latter Days

after Andrew Marvell

Had we but world enough, and time,
your coyness, Sheila, were no crime.
You claim that being chaste is wise,
but open up your pretty eyes
and use your lovely head to think.
This globe is poised upon the brink;
the end of days is coming fast—
extinction by a fission blast,
for war now comes atomic size
and Armageddon's on the rise.
As final judgment gathers speed
no savior waits to intercede
and rectify things from above.
There is no time to wait for love.
The tick of time's a tolling bell;
we're on the downward slope to hell.
We can, however, cheat our fate.
It's not too hopeless or too late.
Let's rob the devil of his due,
reduce the casualties by two.
Let's exit from this doomsday road,
secure ourselves a snug abode,
and fuck until we both explode.

Apologia Pro Vita Sua

on Christian Ward plagiarizing a poem by Helen Mort

It little profits that an idle ~~king~~ poet
Should say: "That is not what I meant at all."
I am a part of all that I have ~~met~~ read
Now recollected in tranquility.
Tho' much is taken, much abides, ~~and though~~ to take.
To strive, to seek, to find, and not to yield.
I am the silence in a snowy field.
The lady doth protest too much, methinks.
Look on my works, ye mighty, and despair.
Tread softly, because you tread on my dreams.
When I am dead, I hope it may be said:
"His sins were scarlet, but his ~~books~~ thefts were read."

The Tavern

after Robert Frost

Tonight I'm going out to drink some beer
And stay, perhaps, to watch the tavern clear.
A corner booth provides a covert view
Of those who catch my eye. —One might be you.

The weekend waitress is so firm and young
I'd like to touch her, taste her with my tongue.
That alley. Or the park she passes through:
I could wait for her. —Or maybe you.

To John, Long Dead

after Donne

Death is not proud. It's punctual.
It's fairly dealt and functional.
Death's not a mimic rest or sleep,
but takes our flesh and soul to keep.
Death is not callous, cruel, or vain
but kindly, modest, and humane.
Death grants complete oblivion,
not misty heavens falsely spun.
Death's not a transient pain, a lie,
nor doomed itself to someday die,
for after death Death's just begun—
not finally finished, ended, done.

Proposition

one more riff on Andrew Marvell

Had we but world enough, and time,
this coyness, Cindy, were no crime.
But life is nasty, brutal, short,
and wanton gods kill us for sport.
The doomsday clock is ticking down;
a missile's aimed right at your town.
You may, the recent tabloids say,
by accident most any day
be poisoned by a mutant toad.
The sun might nova and explode;
a falling safe could crush your head.
See what I mean? You're good as dead.
You're quickly running out of luck.
We'd better hurry up and fuck.

Existential

after Walt Whitman

Out of that cradle endlessly rocking
we come to the world with a slap and a cry.
Leaving this life is equally shocking—
back to the cradle without knowing why.

Common Passage

after Emily Dickinson

I did not care to stop for death,
But still he came and stopped for me
And took as fare my final breath—
All I was—All I'd ever be.

VI

The Other Side of Us

The Other Side of Us

"What then do you call your soul? What idea have you of it?"
—Voltaire

I
Where does one begin?

God's creative breath
inhaled at birth, exhaled at death

a flicker of eternity
wrapped loosely in your skin

another word for what we are—
the dust from an exploded star

the fusion of a sperm and egg,
a mutant strand of DNA

the last of you to slip away
when on your final leg

the *you* in you, the *me* in me—
the stamp of personality

a handy peg
on which to hang
the hope of immortality

II

And what should we presume?

an extramundane self,
a shade, a wraith
an article of faith

his empty chair, *her* vacant room
that urn of ashes on a shelf

the *elf* inside an *I*

the feeling that you will not die—
even if you want to,
even if you try

reason's counterweight

a matter of debate—
what clerics preach about
and skeptics doubt

it frames two windows in the eyes
for looking in and looking out

III

perhaps it's what we gather in—
the sum of everything we've been
a whole that's greater than the parts

or maybe something that you make—
the story of your passing through,
the music of your being here

a reservoir of what we are—
the cistern of our consciousness
collecting run-off from the world,
filling up deep down in us

IV

Skinner's box, Pavlov's bell

a lesson learned in Sunday school
along with angels, heaven, hell
commandments and the golden rule

something very mystical
medieval, alchemical

a heaven baited hook
to catch the gullible

the lone survivor of your sinking ship
fastened on a lifeline to hereafter

a mystic's inward holiday,
the nonbeliever's laughter

a damned elusive thing—

when in pursuit of it, you find yourself
caught squarely in a roundabout
chasing ancient archetypes,
reaching for a golden ring

a candle flame that won't snuff out

a fictive suit of clothes
designed to shroud oblivion

V

a number: 21

its mass as measured out in grams
by Dr. D. MacDougall once
at Dorchester Consumptives' Home,
a mansion turned into a sanitarium—
a pretty place to die, that stately house
with porticoes opening to a view
of tree-lined Blue Hill Avenue—

and there upon a bed-made-scale
the doctor meant to calculate
the slight ethereal weight
a person's body lost at death—

the patient did his part and died,
and with his final breath
a hummingbird in heft
(about three quarters of an ounce)

winged away and left
the mortal bulk behind—

a singular experiment,
an insubstantial find

VI

Hillman's acorn, Hamlet's ghost
the Virgin Mary, full of grace,
appearing on a piece of toast

Plato's daemon, Vishnu's dream
the mystery beneath the face
that molds a Mona Lisa smile

reflections in a funhouse mirror

what animists see everywhere—
in rat and tree and rock and stream

a carrot for the rank and file,
a notion more or less in style
depending on the current trend

one way for us to play pretend

a consolation prize
for all the pleasure life denies

to talk about, poetic—
believing in, absurd

a very funny concept,
but such a lovely word

VII

sometimes we watch it go,
see it leaving—
hear a voice pronounce it dead

like a hammer blow, quick and blunt

or slow, like rising steam,
a trailing plume, a thread
that dissipates at dusk
until it's gone, dissolved in air,
no longer here or anywhere

leaving behind an empty husk
and maybe someone grieving

VIII

passionate, pedantic
overly dramatic,
some speak of it with rapture
in cloudy psycho-blabber—

they ferret out and capture
the deeply esoteric
and claim to comprehend
its origin and end—

like searchers for the Grail
they're classically romantic
and borderline fanatic
when hot upon the trail

IX

Now I lay me down to sleep ...

and if you wake at night
when the swoosh of the wind in the trees
rustles the leaves like rain,
and long white curtains billow out
and then draw back again
against the screens,
and moonlight bars a windowpane—

that way you feel
while lying quiet and alone,
awake and wordless in the dark

maybe that is what it means
or when it seems most real—

X

a philosophic trick or treat
your deepest pain, your sharpest pleasure

that place where Self and Other meet

the myriad workings of the mind—
something science can't define,
isolate, or measure

our quiddities as told in fable,
the medium that moves a séance table

your *being* wide awake

a curse, a crutch, a choice
the echo of an inner voice

a metaphysical mistake

a dance of quarks, a quantum flux
(the lover's kiss you can't forget)
neurons triggered in the brain
{a transcendental empty set}

XI

some remnant bits of you
thrown back into the subatomic soup

a transmigrating force
that comes and goes and comes again
inside an endless loop...

another way of knowing
the other side of us

the Veil of Maya lifted—
our understanding shaken,
our way of seeing shifted

the underside of seem—
the realm of dream

protoplasm grown aware—
ruminating on itself

handprints on a cave wall at Lascaux
a Mass by Bach, a rhapsody by Liszt

your being here, your letting go—

something in your life you missed

XII
implausible inheritance,
birthright guaranteed

the phantom cargo in your hold,

potential's buried seed

an immaterial twin,
a doppelgänger housed within—

it haunts the attic in your heart,
the basement of your mind

amorphous, thin as air—
an apparition ill-defined,
but always with you, always there

your body's spectral friend

hanging on until the end

VII

Eclipses

Time's Arrow

The law of entropy
says all things fall apart:
so goes a galaxy,
a nation-state, the heart.

The Golden Age

Phidias, again and again
as master of the marble arts,
carved statues of bare naked men
that showed in public private parts.

Weird Socrates just loafed around
and pestered people with his tongue—
contesting every rule he found,
corrupting both the old and young.

And ribald Aristophanes
got laughs with sex and vulgar jokes.
His plays laced with obscenities
aroused the coarse and common folks.

Epicurus, that carnal sage
and sybarite who spurned the gods,
made *carpe diem* all the rage
and reveled long against the odds.

And so it went, Greek after Greek,
those rascals running on and on
until they reached a pagan peak
and tumbled headlong and were gone.

Thus time eclipsed that antique past,
that savage, rude, and heathen race
whose aberrations could not last
but perished, leaving little trace.

Still, there are some who sing their praise,
who rave and never cease to speak
of godlike men and golden days,
extolling everything that's Greek.

Not Yet

This late August night
crickets chirp incessantly,
their shrill chorus
slicing through the porch screens
as easily as heat or moonlight or memory.

Her bedroom window,
black as Minnesota soil,
rectangles low on the wall
a body length beyond my chair.
She's quiet now.

At eighty-seven she has little left that works:
bad eyes, bad back,
bad stomach, bad heart.
Not even the bed and toilet give comfort these days.
She's worn out and wants to die.

I don't know how the crickets sound to her
in her sleep, if she should hear them.
To me they repeat a single metallic phrase,
squeaking like a rusty two-note hinge:
not yet, not yet, not yet—

Maya Blue

In time there's nothing left to do
but yield and pay the bloody price,
like someone smeared with Maya blue
and offered as a sacrifice
by hands that split the chest apart
and rip from it a beating heart.

François Villon: The Last Testament

I am François from Paris, France,
admitted brawler, vagrant, thief—
somewhat by choice, more so by chance
when born to poverty and grief.

I loved the woman Isabeau
but lost her to a cleric's lust.
I moved among the mean and low,
both felt and dealt a dagger-thrust.

I stole from churches, killed a priest.
My life's been reckless, violent, loose—
arrested, tortured, then released
I barely slipped the hangman's noose.

With small remorse for all my sins
I haunted squalid city streets,
sang bawdy songs in sleazy inns,
kept company with rogues and cheats.

I've known the dismal country lanes,
the underbelly of a town,
the human wreckage that remains
when souls are crushed and broken-down.

I always drew suspicious looks
and lived with hunger, filth, and fear.
I sought relief in words and books
and mused on snows of yesteryear.

The birthmark of iniquity
stains mortal man since Adam's fall,
and death's the common destiny
for everyone, both great and small.

Among the highborn and refined
who live in luxury and silk
are greater sinners than my kind
and blacker villains than my ilk.

Now judgment grips me by the balls
and only God can grant reprieve,
but mercy's silent, darkness falls,
and hope rolls up an empty sleeve.

I ran again to save my life
and broke my mother's heart once more.
I fled from known to unknown strife
and disappeared at thirty-four.

Led by a dancing skeleton
I trod the pilgrim's road to hell
that drops behind a setting sun
where gravely tolls a vesper bell.

I leave a legacy of shame,
egregious debts too steep to pay,
a crime and murder tarnished name,
some verses sure to fade away.

Vacancy

yellow leaves
gather in
a dry birdbath

crowd together
like empty
chairs waiting

for someone
to come sit
down and wait

for something

Such Stuff

I dream a dream I know I've dreamt before.
Once out of sleep I can't recall the scene.
All light is lost behind a closing door.

Recurring waves which lap a common shore
recede without my knowing what they mean.
I dream a dream I'm sure I dreamt before.

Those shadowed eyes I've searched, but see no more,
extinguish now as if they'd never seen
the light that's lost behind the closing door.

Whose slender arm that gestures like an oar?
Whose face with lips that whisper, part, and lean
into this dream that I have dreamt before?

Like slippered feet that fade across a floor,
like flour sifting through a metal screen,
all light is lost behind a closing door.

I walk an empty, endless corridor
or stand in silence by a dark ravine
in this same dream that I have dreamt before,
until the final closing of the door.

Wakan Song

for Nathan Vandewege (1981–2008)

Listen,
and you will hear him speak.
He's always fastened in your heart,
always near as a thought in you.
And now, a ranging spirit, he's part
of the native world he loved and knew.

Listen.
He will speak to you.

When you are sorrowful and weak,
when anguish grinds you raw,
then listen, listen to him speak.
You'll hear him in a springtime thaw
as rivulets of melting snow
race down a hill and chuckle into streams.

Listen.
You'll hear him in the laughing wind,
the cawing of a shaman crow,
the warble of a purple finch.

Listen,
and he will talk.

He'll speak to you
in the silhouette of a red-tailed hawk
that floats and circles through a summer sky.
And from those wings against the vaulted blue,
those lifting wings that lead your eye
beyond the tragedies of earth,
in such a moment, he will speak to you.

Listen.

Hearsay

A wind—on good authority—
informed a flagging leaf,
which whispered to a vagrant bee
to rumor never deaf—

from softly spoken butterflies
the word discreetly went,
with mute efficiency of touch
it passed from ant to ant—

then stumbled on a somber stone
that told an idle bird—
another man has gone to bone,
the prairie grass has heard.

90 Years, 4 Months, 12 Days

Late Sunday afternoon,
halfway through
her three days of dying,
a flock of crows arched over the house,
their large black wings rowing
against a gray October sky.

They settled in the trees
of neighboring yards, perched
high in the branches.
Some called out *kahr kahr kahr*,
others answered
caw caw caw.

They stayed awhile,
then flew off.

The crows came
to take my mother away.
She lay on her back,
nearly naked,
the sheets kicked from the bed,
pillows pushed to the floor.

She lay in dim light, eyes
open and glazed, lips
fluttering with labored breathing.
Thin arms lifted from her chest,
flapped weakly above her.
Her hands pecked the air like beaks.

Epistemology

"The meaning of life is that it stops." —Franz Kafka

For all the knowledge learned men dispense,
Their labored arguments and strained defense,
 Inside this labyrinth where all are lost
The deepest wisdom's cemetery sense.

Leaving the tangled talk and keen debate
About this maze of life we label Fate,
 My shuffling footsteps whisper in the dust:
The end of every path's a graveyard gate.

Mallard

o

v

V

V

V V V V V
V V V
V

*

K/iiii

V V V   V
V V V
V

An Old Docent Dreams of Museums

Now having loitered through the gallery
and vacantly observed what painters see
displayed like timeworn posters on a wall:
a nude descending in a golden fall,
a pleasant portrait of a mademoiselle,
a pair of pretty lovers painted well,
two ancient armies warring on a plain,
a crucifixion lacking blood and pain,
a bowl of fruit beside an empty glass,
some people lounging on a stretch of grass,
a splash of colors in a brilliant smear,
an enigmatic girl, abstract and queer,
lithe dancers resting on a sunlit floor,
and all the many others, many more...

Regard a while *The Fall of Icarus.*

A window on the world, it mirrors us
and offers you, the thoughtful passer-by,
a chance to see your death before you die.

Resplendent in repose the raptured world
reveals a panorama poised and pearled.
The plowman plies his leather lash,
unnoticed goes the meager splash.
A shepherd squints into the sky,
his back turned toward a muffled cry,

and neither sheep nor dogs can scent
the death so near and imminent.
Beneath a bright congenial sun,
oblivious, a fisherman
sits angling on the rocky beach
while near at hand, almost in reach,
two scissored legs kick helplessly
and disappear into the sea.
A splendid ship adorns the bay
as life is lost an oar away.
Here nothing startles earth or sea or sky
as wonted ways go calmly on and by.

Thus Brueghel with the master's art and ease
sagaciously transcends the centuries
and shows you though you may not know or care
just how you are while there you stand and stare:
in life a mote, decreasing by degrees,
ignored and meager in your miseries,
among the multitude a single groan,
condemned to suffer, suffer—all alone.

Ancient History

She made a Carthage of my heart
then salted it and plowed
and left no word upon a word
of all that she had vowed.

Her chronicles expunge the name,
her maps blot out the place.
A truth, a past, a slaughtered love
are easy to erase.

Armageddon

The plot concludes with World War III,
a paradisal victory.
Though hell may do its uttermost,
it's the father, son, and holy ghost
on whom the faithful must depend
to fabricate a fitting end.

The Autumn Way

for Gertrude Klugherz Meyer (1917–2007)

Resigning to their autumn fate,
The last few leaves release their grip.
Without objection or debate
Willing branches let them slip
    And drift away like yellow wings.
    Such is the autumn way of things.

The robins left long weeks ago
Without a farewell look or song.
They always have the wit to know
It's time for them to move along.
    Something inward tells them so.
    They recognize the need to go.

The wind announces winter's near
And revels in the icy news.
And then, as if I did not hear
That there's so little time to lose,
    It whistles louder and more clear:
    "Winter's near! Winter's near!"

Some see a message in the fall
When birds depart and leaves descend.
They say the lesson for us all
Is everything will have an end.
    I understand both bird and tree.
    Their lesson is not lost on me.

But we must still account for will.
I've lived too long to be dismayed
By autumn loss and winter chill,
Yet considerations must be weighed
When on some late autumnal day
The mind says *go* and the heart says *stay*.

One day I'll follow leaf and bird
And take the breezy autumn way.
I'll be both willing and assured.
I'll not object, I'll not delay.
I'll recognize my time to go
When something inward tells me so.

Wheatfield with Crows

after the painting by Vincent van Gogh

a field of yellow grief
pressed by an iron sky—
pain applied impasto

roads wind from nowhere
to nothing—snipped short,
blunt and abrupt, like cut rope

and the crows coming in—
dark hinges dropping low
over the troubled grain

sinister wedges, black Vs
scribbled beyond the horizon,
stuttering to say your name

and their rusty voices
striking like clods of dirt—
mocking *van caw, van caw*

No sunflowers flourish here.

Well-Attended

After the funeral they stop by
the house for lunch, an open buffet
for backyard feeders: mourning doves,
black-capped chickadees, goldfinches,
grosbeaks, nuthatches.
                                        Sparrows belly up
to the birdbath, make room
for a stray starling on the rim.
Grackles pace the green lawn
like dark-suited ushers.
                                        A cardinal
pulses red on a bent pine limb, drops in
like a blood clot, calls out
what-cheer, what-cheer cheer cheer
gertie gertie gertie
as if you were here, behind that gray screen,
whistling in your chair on the sunlit porch.

Swagman

When paper-shuffler death
comes mincing in the room
to settle up affairs

I'll push aside the earth
and rise above the moon
and set out for the stars

unlodged from doubt and faith,
light traveling on my own
with love's red-shifted scars.

Acknowledgments

My deepest appreciation goes to Amy Malecki Rogers, my editor and publisher. She made it possible for my dream of a book to appear in the three-dimensional world. My gratitude for her generosity, talent, and creativity is beyond saying.

I also wish to thank the editors of the journals and periodicals in which the following poems first appeared, sometimes in slightly different versions:

14 Magazine	"Dimmicks Beach," "A Life"
Able Muse	"Communion," "Well-Attended"
Alabama Literary Review	"No Sanctuary"
Angle	"Adrift," "The Great Builders," "Singularity," "Time's Arrow," "Anima," "Indian Summer," "Fault Line," "Ancient History," "The Mongrel," "The Go-Around," "Disputation"
Autumn Sky	"Wheatfield with Crows"
The Classical Outlook	"Sisyphus"
The Evansville Review	"Fieldstone"
The Flea	"Swagman"
Light	"To Eva, Who Clings To Chastity," "Blind Date," "Proposition," "The Descent of Man"

Measure	"The Penitent," "October Closing," "Waist Deep," "To Helen, A Working Girl at *The Palace*," "La Gioconda"
New Verse News	"*Apologia Pro Vita Sua*"
Per Contra	"Quandary," "First Cause"
The Raintown Review	"Something Like Worms"
Shit Creek Review	"Solicitation: Love in the Latter Days," "Altar Call"
String Poet	"The Autumn Way," "This Morning," "Sunday Morning in June"
Think	"Passer Domesticus"

Be a poetry advocate!

Share your thoughts on *Orbital Paths* at your favorite
social media, or the book sites:

GoodReads
Barnes & Noble
amazon
Apple iBooks

Visit Richard Meyer on Facebook
https://www.facebook.com/groups/2215533802/

This beautiful book crafted by the publishing artisans at

 ScienceThrillers Media

Contact:
publisher@ScienceThrillersMedia.com

ScienceThrillers Media specializes in both fiction and
popular nonfiction books with themes of science,
technology, engineering, mathematics, or medicine.

Visit our website and join the STM mailing list to learn
about new releases.

ScienceThrillersMedia.com

About the Poet

*A*lthough he has written poetry for most of his adult life, Richard Meyer didn't begin sending his work out for publication until after concluding a thirty-two-year career as a teacher of high school English and humanities. In addition to his poems appearing in a variety of print and online journals, Meyer was awarded the 2012 Robert Frost Farm Prize for his poem "Fieldstone" and was the recipient of the 2014 String Poet Prize for his poem "The Autumn Way." His poetry has also received top honors in the Great River Shakespeare Festival sonnet contest.

As a result of the recognition he's received in recent years, Meyer may be identified in some literary circles as a significant emerging poet. Given his age, Richard says he is "delighted to have emerged before being interred."

Richard lives in his family home, the house his father built, in Mankato, a city at the bend of the Minnesota River. Born in 1951, he is the third of eight children of Andy and Gertrude (Klugherz) Meyer.

Orbital Paths is Richard Meyer's first book of collected poems.

Photo by John Cross / The Mankato Free Press

CPSIA information can be obtained at www.ICGtesting.com
Printed in the USA
BVOW08s1248181015

422988BV00008B/290/P